Gary Gentile Productions
P.O. Box 57137
Philadelphia, PA 19111

Additional copies of this book may be purchased from the same address by sending a check or money order in the amount of $30 U.S. for each copy (plus $3 for shipping). For information about consulting services, workshops, presentations, and a list of available titles that can be ordered online and paid by credit card, visit the GGP website:

http://www.ggentile.com

Picture Credits

All uncredited photographs were taken by the author. The photographs on the front cover show the alligator figurehead on the *Dunderberg*, the bell on the *Detroit*, the helm and stand on the *Mary Alice B.*, and the ram's head figurehead on the *St. James*. The back cover photograph of the author was taken by Pete Manchee. The photograph on the opposite page shows deadeyes on the *Cornelia B. Windiate*.

International Standard Book Number (ISBN) 1-883056-13-6

First Edition

Printed in Hong Kong

PREAMBLE

I have often declared that the Great Lakes possess the best shipwrecks in the world. The purist might take exception to this statement by observing that I have not dived everywhere in the world. The purist would be correct. I have dived on shipwrecks along the eastern seaboard of the United States and Canada, in the St. Lawrence River and Seaway, in Bermuda, in the Caribbean, in the United Kingdom (England, Ireland, and Scotland), in Australia, and in the South Pacific. This may seem like a broad representation, but in reality there is more of the world in which I have *not* dived than there is of the world in which I *have*. Nonetheless, I maintain that my claim is valid because I have read about and seen photographs of wrecks in the rest of the world, in books and magazines. The combination of my own experiences and these vicarious ramblings has led me to the conclusion that is declared in the first sentence.

What is more in contention in my declaration is: what do I mean by "best"? From my primary perspective as an underwater explorer, I define "best" as "the most spectacular to behold." Compared to aged saltwater wrecks, which have been demolished by deep ocean swells and by the natural deterioration that has resulted from the corrosive briny environment in which they sank, freshwater wrecks possess far more recognizable form. Most ocean wrecks are compacted, with little structure remaining and with few identifiable features. Teredoes and other wood-boring organisms have eaten the exposed wooden hulls and planks; ferrous metal beams and plates have been reduced to rusty, brittle components; the parts that abide are thickly encrusted with marine fouling organisms such as barnacles, sea anemones, hydroids, coral, kelp, and the like. By contrast, until the recent invasion by zebra mussels, Great Lakes wrecks may be so "clean" that the grain in the wood is clearly discernible.

From a secondary viewpoint as a photographer, I quantify "best" as "the most photogenic." Wrecks that are fundamentally intact (by comparison to their seawater brethren) offer a great deal more subject matter to capture on film. By contrast, interesting photos can be difficult to obtain on wrecks that exist merely as flattened junk heaps that are completely festooned with organic growth. But in the Great Lakes, shipwrecks are sometimes like museum pieces, exhibiting portholes, deadeyes, gauges, chinaware, legible name boards, even ornate figureheads. These are attractions that will entice any shipwreck photographer worth his "salt."

From a tertiary standpoint as an historian, some of the "best" wrecks are those that were yesteryear's most tragic. Their fascination lies in their sad sagas of shipwreck and survival, dramatic rescues, and the melancholy circumstances of impending death. Furthermore, many Great Lakes wrecks are historic by dint of their age and methods of construction. The diversity of shipwreck *types* is clearly substantial, so that anyone interested in the structure of vessels and their evolution will find a wealth of material to study.

There is a common misconception that shipwrecks in the Great Lakes are preserved in perpetuity, that they will maintain their present condition forever. Anyone who has dived on these wrecks knows otherwise. Granted, the hulls are better protected and more intact than their seaside equivalents; but they are by no means perfectly preserved as if they existed in a vacuum. It is more precise to state that the rate of deterioration is greatly reduced than to state that it has been halted forever. Nothing abides in stasis. In that wise, this book performs the function of preserving in photographic format the images that future generations will be denied.

The shipwrecks depicted in the following pages are the ones that have impressed me the most, in accordance with the criteria given above.

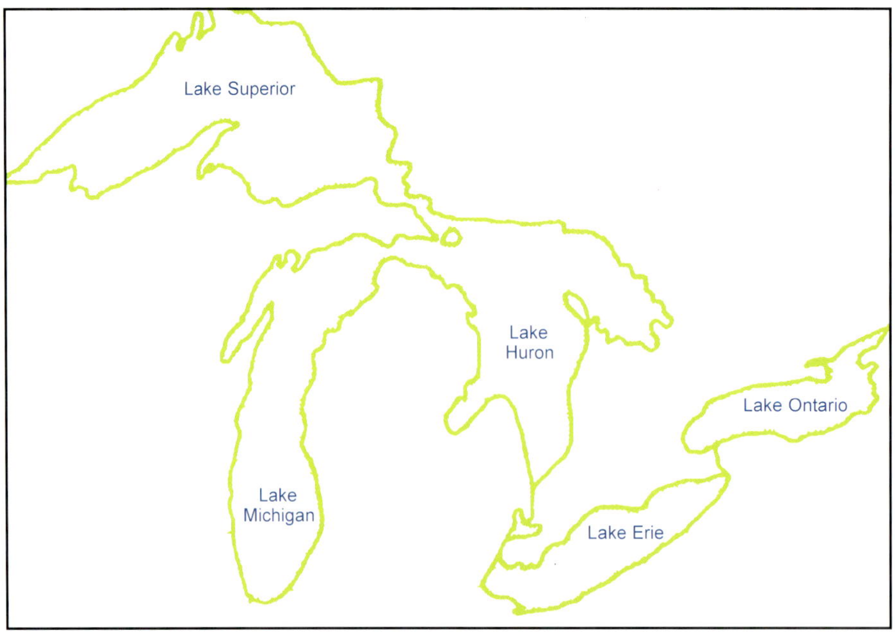

Great Lakes Shipwrecks
a Photographic Odyssey

by Gary Gentile

GARY GENTILE PRODUCTIONS
P.O. Box 57137
Philadelphia, PA 19111
2003

CONTENTS

Isle Royale — Page 6
America - 1898 to 1928 June 7 — Page 8
Emperor - 1910 to 1947 June 4 — Page 10
Kamloops - 1924 to 1927 December 6 — Page 12

Lake Superior — Page 14
Barge 115 - 1891 to 1899 December 18 — Page 16
Bermuda - 1860 to 1883 October ? — Page 17
Columbus - 1874 to 1909 September 10 — Page 18
Gray Oak - 1885 to 1911 ? — Page 20
John B. Cowle - 1902 to 1909 July 12 — Page 22
John M. Osborn - 1882 to 1884 July 27 — Page 24
Rappahannock - 1895 to 1911 July 25 — Page 26
Samuel Mather - 1887 to 1891 November 22 — Page 28
St. Andrew - 1885 to 1900 September 21 — Page 30
Vienna - 1873 to 1892 September 17 — Page 32

Lake Michigan — Page 34
Lady Elgin - 1851 to 1860 September 8 — Page 36
Rotarian - 1889 to 1931 September 28 — Page 38
Wells Burt - 1873 to 1893 February 2 — Page 39

Straits of Mackinac — Page 40
Sandusky - 1848 to 1856 September 20 — Page 41

North Channel — Page 42
North Wind - 1888 to 1926 July 1 — Page 43

Georgian Bay — Page 44
Arabia - 1853 to 1884 October 4 — Page 45
City of Grand Rapids - 1879 to 1907 October 29 — Page 46
Sweepstakes - 1867 to 1885 August — Page 47

Lake Huron — Page 48

Cornelia B. Windiate - 1874 to 1875 November ? — Page 50
Detroit - 1846 to 1854 May 25 — Page 54
Dunderberg - 1867 to 1868 August 13 — Page 56
Florida - 1889 to 1897 May 20 — Page 58
F. T. Barney - 1856 to 1868 October 23 — Page 62
Goliath - 1846 to 1851 November 3 — Page 65
Grecian - 1891 to 1906 June 7 — Page 66
Hercules - 1904 to 1932 December 23 — Page 70
Hunter Savidge - 1879 to 1899 August 20 — Page 71
James R. Bentley - 1867 to 1878 November 12 — Page 72
John J. Audubon - 1854 to 1854 October 20 — Page 74
Mary Alice B. - 1931 to 1975 September 5 — Page 77
Metropole - 1883 to 1903 August 8 — Page 78
Monrovia - 1943 to 1959 June 25 — Page 81
Newell A. Eddy - 1890 to 1893 April 20 — Page 84
Perseverance - 1855 to 1864 November 24 — Page 86
Regina - 1907 to 1913 November 10-13 — Page 88
Typo - 1873 to 1899 October 14 — Page 90
Viator - 1904 to 1935 October 31 — Page 91

Lake Erie — Page 93

Carlingford - 1869 to 1881 November 12 — Page 94
Crystal Wreck - Unknown — Page 95
Dean Richmond - 1864 to 1893 August 14 — Page 96
John J. Boland, Jr. - 1928 to 1932 October 5 — Page 97
Oxford - 1842 to 1856 May 30 — Page 98
Smith - 1881 to 1930 October 25 — Page 100
St. James - 1856 to 1870 October ? — Page 101
Success - 1790 (or 1840) to 1946 July 4 — Page 102

Lake Ontario — Page 103

Annie Falconer - 1867 to 1904 November 12 — Page 104
City of Sheboygan - 1871 to 1915 September 25 — Page 105
J. H. Munson - ? to 1890 April 30 — Page 108
Manola - 1890 to 1918 December 3 — Page 109
Olive Branch - 1871 to 1880 September 30 — Page 111

Books by the Author — Page 112

ISLE ROYALE

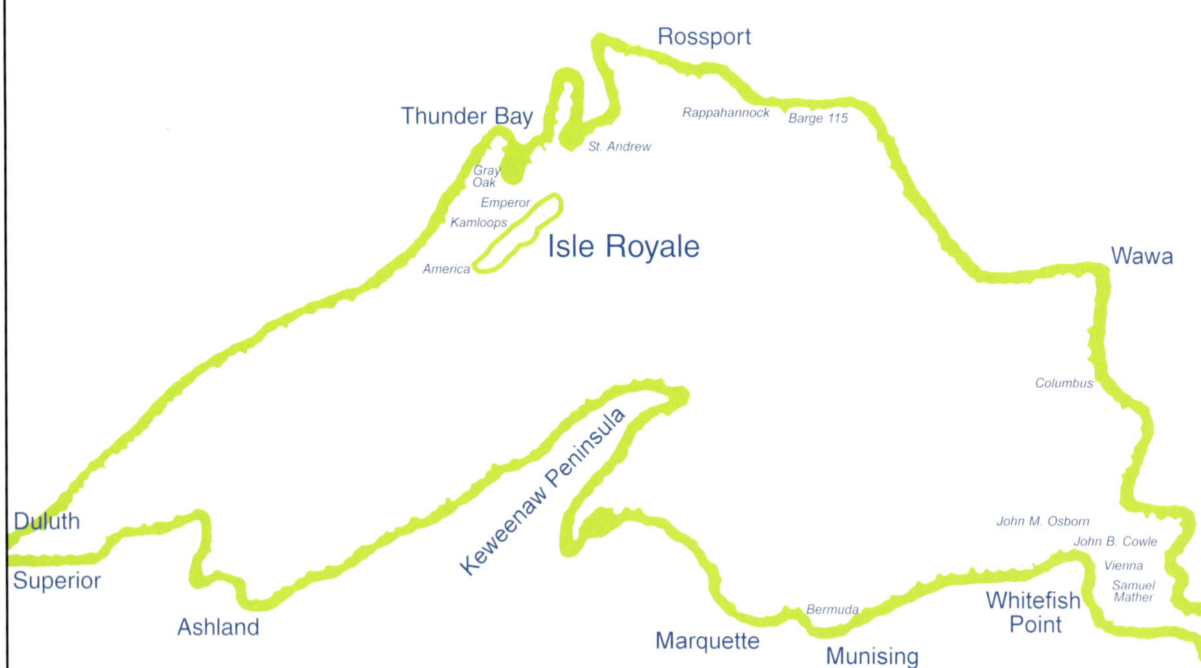
Rossport
Thunder Bay
Rappahannock
Barge 115
St. Andrew
Gray Oak
Emperor
Kamloops
Isle Royale
America
Wawa
Columbus
Keweenaw Peninsula
Duluth
Superior
Ashland
John M. Osborn
John B. Cowle
Vienna
Samuel Mather
Whitefish Point
Bermuda
Marquette
Munising

Isle Royale consists of a single massive island that is surrounded by numerous unnamed islets and jagged rocks. The main island measures some 40 miles in length; its breadth varies, extending 9 miles at its widest point. This remote island group is nestled in the far northwest corner of Lake Superior. The closest point of land is in Ontario. The second nearest mainland is in Minnesota. Yet the waters surrounding this collection of islands lie within the jurisdiction of Michigan (which is more than twice as far away as Minnesota), while Isle Royale itself is administered by the National Park Service.

If I were to describe Isle Royale in a single word, that word would be "wilderness." I have seen moose and fox, and I am told that wolves and bears may sometimes be sighted. A multitude of birds flit through a pristine forest jammed with birch and aspen, spruce and fir.

Most divers reach the island by private boat, then camp for several days.

Top: Moon over Rock Harbor.
Above: Stacy Ehorn displays her catch: two tasty great northern pike that were plucked out of an upland lake.
Upper left: Moss, lichen, and ferns have completely overgrown this ancient cemetary.
Lower left: Cris Kohl and Don Edwards are wondering how we are going to fit all that dive gear, clothing, camping equipment, and four divers into Don's little boat for the crossing to Isle Royale. Somehow we did it!
Below: A rustic lean-to and a secluded dock.

America

1898 to 1928 June 7
182 feet in length
Steel-hulled passenger vessel
Maximum depth is 85 feet

Top: The American flag is painted on the engine casing beneath the catwalk.
Above: The bow as seen from below the surface.
Above right: The bow as seen from above the surface.
Right: The engine appears as if it were scrubbed and painted yesterday.

The *America* is Isle Royale's most popular shipwreck. The intact hull lies on a slope in shallow water that is normally bright and clear. Stairwells and open hatches beckon divers to explore the dark compartments and silty interior corridors.

Above: Joyce Hayward exiting the forward hatch.
Top right: The midship superstructure.
Right: The stairwell that leads to the compartments below deck.
Bottom right: The fantail in silhouette.
Below: The propeller and rudder jammed in the mud.

Emperor

1910 to 1947 June 4
525 feet in length
Steel-hulled bulk freighter
Maximum depth is 175 feet

The identity of this shipwreck is not in doubt: the name is printed on both the fantail (above) and the nameboard (left). Note the thick hawsers that are draped across the anchor in the adjacent photos below. The bottom right photo shows the entrance to the engine room.

The *Emperor's* compartments are most exciting to explore.
Above left: The light from my strobe reflects off the mirror's silver backing. I did not drink the water.
Above right: Bunk beds in the crew's quarters.
Left: Cookware perched on the galley stove.
Below: This ventilator is large enough for Joyce Hayward to fit inside.

The *Kamloops* is a spooky wreck. It lies at such a depth that sunlight seldom penetrates to the deepest part of the hull: the bow, which rests on the bottom at 260 feet. Because the wreck lies on a slope, the stern rises as high as 180 feet.

Left: I captured this eerie black and white image by dropping beneath the overhanging stern and shooting upward.
Above left: The auxiliary steering helm.
Above right: The compass binnacle, immediately forward of the helm.

Opposite top: A porthole located on the promenade deck is accentuated by the strobe light, which dispels a bit of the gloom.
Opposite center: A sounding machine leaning against the telegraph stand.
Opposite bottom: The docking telegraph.

Kamloops

1924 to 1927 December 6
250 feet in length
Steel-hulled package freighter
Maximum depth is 260 feet

LAKE SUPERIOR

Lake Superior is the biggest body of fresh water in the world. Its dark green surface encompasses more than 31,000 square miles, making it larger in area than all four of the other Great Lakes combined, and larger than eleven of the fifty United States. If this statistic is difficult to accept, try driving around the lake's circumference - plan several days to complete the thousand-mile trip.

Ice Age glaciers scoured the bedrock to a depth of more than 1,300 feet. Gross geological features are seldom affected by water level. If tall cliffs march along the edge of a lake, similar cliffs can be expected to exist under water. So it is with Lake Superior. As a result, water that wreck-divers consider deep is often found close to shore.

To imagine how abrupt underwater drop-offs can be, note the sheer wall that is depicted in the photo at upper left. This sight is typical along the rugged north shore. The people standing at the water's edge are observing the Native American pictograph that is shown above.

Tides in the Great Lakes are barely perceptible, but the water exhibits motion known as seiches, "which are caused by differences in barometric pressure at various points on the Lakes' enormous surfaces and which, once started, can oscillate from end to end of a Lake for days, like water sloshing in a bathtub."

I experienced this curious effect while exploring a shallow creek on one of the north shore's many islands. So much water was carried out of the creek in half an hour that Wally Peterson's raft was left high and dry (see photo above), and we had to carry it several hundred feet to where it would float. The porcupine (right) and the grouse (opposite page, top left) did not seem to mind either the seiche or the photographer.

The shores of Lake Superior are rockbound and craggy. Along the north coast road the land is sparsely inhabited, and communities are few and far between. A motorist may drive a hundred miles between gas stations.

The south shore is not as distant from civilization, but the geological features are every bit as rugged. One of the more scenic areas is known as the Pictured Rocks (photo at right, with boat). Erosion has created many cavernlike indents. The waterfall shown at upper right pours a bounteous supply of cold fresh water into the lake.

The two bottom photos depict the Great Lakes Shipwreck Museum, at Whitefish Point - a must stop for any shipwreck explorer visiting the area.

See page 6 for a map that shows the wreck sites.

Barge 115

1891 to 1899 December 18
256 feet in length
Steel-hulled whaleback
Maximum depth is 80 feet

Mixed metaphors notwithstanding, Alexander McDougall's unique hull design was called both a "whaleback" and a "pigboat." The whaleback allusion was based upon the curvature of the hull: the upper sides sloped inward to form the deck. The pigboat pejorative referred to the distinctive stem that resembled a hog's blunt, rounded snout.

Barge 115 affords a rare opportunity to see these unconventional configurations in clear water. The photo at upper left depicts the swinelike bow from the outside, while the photo at upper right shows the same from the inside. Paint still abides on the interior planking. Note the rusty chain links on the pulley assembly.

The inhospitable shore is shown at lower right. Ryan LeBlanc drew my attention to chunks of steel plate that were wedged in crevices more than forty feet above water level. This wreckage was tossed that high by storm-driven waves.

Below, a diver swims above the intact forward deck.

The *Bermuda* is not necessarily photogenic when compared to the many other prime examples of wooden-hulled sailing vessels that populate the bottomlands of the Great Lakes. But the shallow depth coupled with the exquisite state of preservation combine to make this wreck entrancing for underwater explorers who have limited diving experience. Because bottom time is not constrained by decompression factors, and because ambient light is resplendent, the site affords a perfect opportunity to observe the fine workmanship of nineteenth-century hull construction.

The hull stands upright on a white sandy bottom that reflects sunlight with the intensity of polished silver. Perch may be found swimming in schools along the top deck. The rudder is distinctive. By entering the holds one can observe the centerboard box and the rough-hewn hanging knees that support the upper planks.

The *Bermuda* should not be overlooked.

Bermuda

1860 to 1883 October ?
136 feet in length
Wooden-hulled schooner
Maximum depth is 30 feet

Above: The end of the road (such as it was).
Left: A close-up of the sign.
Below: The trail to the wreck site.

One of my most memorable dives in the Great Lakes involved the *Columbus* - not because of the wreck's historic significance, nor the unlimited bottom time available for exploration, nor the crystal clear water, but because of the challenges presented by accessing the site. Do not confuse "memorable" with "enjoyable."

The *Columbus* burned and sank in a remote corner of the lake known as Gargantua Harbor. Once a thriving fishing village, the harbor has long been bereft of permanent residents, and is now visited infrequently by people seeking solitude in wilderness surroundings.

Ten miles of dirt road separate the harbor from the highway. This road is rough and rocky, deeply rutted, badly washboarded, and hilly. I drove along this wagon trail with Joyce Hayward and Cris Kohl. One stream we had to ford, while several others we crossed by means of decrepit, rotted planks that some wiseacre humorously called bridges. We reached the end of the trail at dusk, cooked out, and camped for the night.

In the morning we learned that further vehicular progress was blocked by a stout metal gate. A barely passable, overgrown dirt trail continued beyond the barricade. We had to walk the rest of the way to the wreck site: a distance that I estimated from the map to be a mile and one third.

I did not own any single tanks, but Cris came to my rescue by loaning me one of his - thus saving me from an arduous trek wearing doubles. Two trips were required. On the first trip I packed a tank in its harness with the regulator connected to the valve, as well as my drysuit and weight belt (which I slung on opposite ends of a thick branch that I balanced on my shoulder). I returned empty handed, then completed the second trip carrying cameras and the remainder of my scuba gear. Thus we hiked four miles before we were ready to take the plunge. Not even a four-wheel-drive vehicle could have negotiated this bridle path.

In true Ciceronean fashion, I will not even mention the debilitating August heat or the bloodthirsty mosquitoes. After the dive we hiked another four miles in reverse order. The tanks weighed less by dint of the compressed air that we had breathed, but that did not come close to compensating for the weight of the water that soaked our gear, and it did nothing to offset the devastating fatigue of a long and arduous day spent imitating pack mules. No wonder mules are so ornery.

But the dive was worth it!

Columbus

1874 to 1909 September 10
136 feet in length
Wooden-hulled steamer
Maximum depth is 25 feet

Top: The engine's cylinder heads protrude above the calm lake surface. After swimming to the wreck and doing a preliminary survey of the site, we perched on the exposed metal edge and discussed how we wanted to compose our photographs, and where the models should take turns posing. Notice the boiler to the left.

Middle: The wreck is shallow enough to snorkel.

Bottom: Evident in the photo are the rudder, rudder post, and tiller arm. One blade of the iron propeller is visible. Notice the bent metal railing on the right.

As the *Superior Sunrise* departed Thunder Bay, Ontario on a three-day cruise to Rockport - to dive wrecks and visit islands along the way - I asked Wally Peterson what we were going to dive first. When he told me the name, I asked him whether the first word was spelled with an "a" or an "e." He thought for a moment, then said that he wasn't sure, but that I could check the spelling because the name was painted on the fantail. This was early in my Great Lakes wreck-diving experience, so I affected disbelief that paint could persist for so long under water. As the reader can see in the photos at the top of the opposite page, my disbelief was soon suspended.

Gray Oak

1885 to 1911 ?
133 feet in length
Wooden-hulled scow
Maximum depth is 95 feet

Even more astonishing than the paint were these unbroken window panes shown at right. The glare of my strobe can be seen at the top of the upper right pane.

Below is a view of the magnificent helm, looking aft.

Right: The inside of the hatch combing shows much of the original paint.

Below: Another view of the helm, looking forward. Joyce Hayward and I took turns posing for each other. Notice the identification tag that is secured to one of the spokes.

John B. Cowle

1902 to 1909 July 12
420 feet in length
Steel-hulled bulk ore carrier
Maximum depth is 220 feet

This postcard picture of the *John B. Cowle* demonstrates how bulk ore carriers were loaded quickly - usually in a few hours. According to design, the ore shoots and the vessel's hatches were spaced identically, so that each hold was filled by its corresponding hopper simultaneously.

Exploration of the intact forward superstructure is exhilarating.
Opposite page top: The helm stand in the wheel house, looking forward. Notice the hanging cable.
Opposite page bottom right: The telegraph pedestal on the flying bridge, at a depth of 180 feet.
Opposite page bottom left: This sink is located in a compartment abaft the wheel house. The drain must be clogged because the sink was filled with water. Wood paneling covers the metal bulkhead.
Above left and right: The outside of the wheel house bulkhead, showing the ladder that extends to the flying bridge, and brass portholes with unbroken glass. Note the thickness of the ferrous oxidation.
Bottom: An officer's cabin. Notice the bed railing in the background.

John M. Osborn

1882 to 1884 July 27
178 feet in length
Wooden-hulled bulk freighter
Maximum depth is 175 feet

Opposite page top left: Absent sections of planking produce a skeletal effect in the stern where the hull is collapsed.
Opposite page top right: The thickness of the wooden bulwark is emphasized by this scupper.
Opposite page bottom: The symbols that appear to be Babylonian cuneiform adorn a metal band around the engine cylinders. The vertical wooden slats encase the cylinder heads.

Top: Crossed anchors on the bow.
Above: Spare blocks in the forecastle. Notice the anchor chain extending through the hawsepipe.
Right: A bilge pump.
Below: A ceramic mug. Notice the large chunks of coal in the background.

Upper left: The *Rappahannock* sank off the pointed cliff that is shown in this historical photo. At the time the picture was taken, a stone railroad jetty was being constructed across the bay. A culvert permits water to flow under the jetty. Part of the fun of diving the *Rappahannock* is reaching the site.

Left: Cris Kohl and Ryan LeBlanc guide an inflatable boat toward the culvert.

Above: The outflow was so shallow that we had to drag the boat.

Below: In the workshop, iron tools hanging on the wooden partition have stained the white paint a rusty red.

Rappahannock

1895 to 1911 July 25
308 feet in length
Wooden-hulled bulk freighter
Maximum depth is 85 feet

Top: Not only was this can of lard remarkably well preserved, but the lard inside was still firm and milky in color.
Right: Iron chains hanging on the outer bulkhead of a compartment, next to a porthole opening.
Below: A lifeboat davit.
Bottom right: A bench vice in the workshop.

Samuel Mather

1887 to 1891 November 22
246 feet in length
Wooden-hulled steam freighter
Maximum depth is 175 feet

Top left: Rusticles are common occurrences on ferrous hulls and machinery in the Great Lakes. They are produced by the bacterial reduction of iron, and form long strips that look much like icicles stained with rust.

Above: Donkey boiler resting in its cradle on deck.

Top: The tip of the bow is broken and the anchor hangs precariously.
Above left: Fife rail (or spider band) around the mast.
Above right: A deadlight amidst the anchor chain and windlass.
Right: Draft marks on the stem.
Opposite bottom left: Wire cables inside the forecastle.
Opposite bottom right: The starboard side of the forecastle. The piping is part of the bilge pump system. Water sucked up the vertical pipe was diverted through the hull and ejected overboard. Notice the intact barrel, complete with wooden staves and metal bands.
Opposite (above bottom right photo): An "exploded" barrel that probably contained a substance that expanded when it got soaked, causing the barrel to rupture.

Although the *St. Andrew* is completely broken down, and the site is sequestered off a deserted isle along the remotest area of Lake Superior's north shore, there is much to see on this shallow wreck that makes a visit well worth the effort to get there. Bright ambient light enhances the experience.

Above, a propeller blade rests atop a wooden handtruck (for the movement of cargo or bags of coal). Another handtruck lies nearby.

Below, both ends of a steam whistle protrude from under a heavy beam that has crushed the whistle in the middle.

St. Andrew

1885 to 1900 September 21
193 feet in length
Wooden-hulled bulk freighter
Maximum depth is 60 feet

Above: A view of the propeller blade and handtrucks looking in the opposite direction of the view on the facing page.
Top right: A bilge pump festooned with algae.
Bottom right: Ornately carved promenade deck posts attest to the vessel's unusual elegance.
Below: The box for the centerboard keel. When approaching the shoals of undeveloped shores, the moveable keel was raised into this watertight well, thus reducing the vessel's draft.

Vienna

1873 to 1892 September 17
191 feet in length
Wooden-hulled bulk freighter
Maximum depth is 150 feet

When I saw the crescent moon carved in the wooden partition, I immediately thought of an outhouse. Sure enough, when I peeped around the corner, there was the toilet! The wooden poles stowed vertically in the rack beneath the crescent are the bars for the capstan, shown above.

At left, the lifeboat resides on the upper deck.

In the photo above, the vertical bar between the rudder and the propeller is the rudder post. The top right photo is a close-up of the rudder post, showing the draft marks painted in Roman numerals.

At right, a burbot swims through a porthole.

Below is the steam whistle.

The photo at bottom right shows the ornately carved eagle that once perched atop the *Vienna's* wheel house. The eagle now resides in the Great Lakes Shipwreck Museum, at Whitefish Point. Tom Farnquist, the museum's founder and curator, recovered many of the relics that are on display.

LAKE MICHIGAN

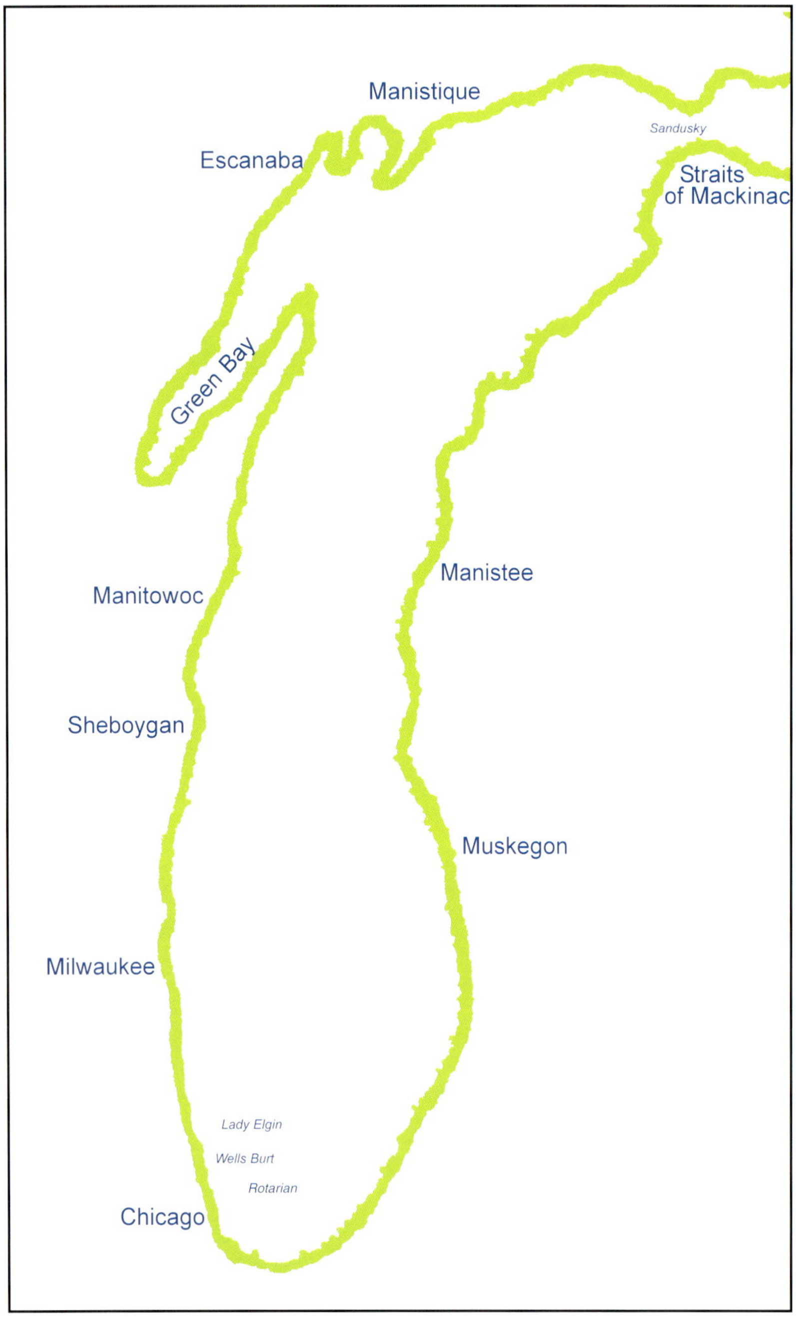

The amount of diving that I have done in Lake Michigan is sadly lacking. Thus, from the paucity of wrecks that are included in this section, the reader might get the impression that the lake has been relatively free from maritime casualty. Such is not the case. There are more shipwrecks in Lake Michigan than meet the eye that views the following pages. Perhaps I will cover more of them in another volume.

Lake Michigan is an area of great disparities. The southern end is quite "citified" with major metropolitan centers (such as Chicago) and invasive industrial development, while the northern end is more sparsely populated and rampant with rugged natural shores that beg for outdoor exploration.

Retreating ice-age glaciers carved the depths, while modern weather continuously shapes the coastlines with endless cycles of sand erosion and deposition. Weather also accounted for many of the shipping casualties, for storms can brew up quickly.

The maximum depth in Lake Michigan is slightly more than 900 feet.

Storms move quickly across Lake Michigan. The one shown in the upper photo occurred off Sheboygan. We dived in the morning under a threatening sky, then raced back to the dock before the tempest burst upon our unprotected boat. This propensity for rapidly developing and swiftly advancing storm cells accounted for many of yesteryear's maritime casualties.

One of the greatest losses to Great Lakes maritime history was the destruction of the *Alvin Clark*. This wooden-hulled hermaphrodite brig was built in 1846, and sank in a storm on June 29, 1864. In 1969, in an incredible feat of salvage, the intact hull of this 113-foot-long vessel was raised from a depth of 110 feet, off Chambers Island in Green Bay, and placed on display in Menominee, Michigan. The entire salvage operation was financed privately.

I was fortunate enough the see the *Alvin Clark* in 1989, before she disintegrated completely. Unable to afford the cost of conservation, and unable to obtain public funding, the owner could not prevent the timbers from desiccating and the hull from crumbling. After collapsing upon itself, the vessel was dismembered and carted off to the trash dump.

LADY ELGIN

1851 to 1860 September 8
252 feet in length
Wooden-hulled passenger sidewheeler
Maximum depth is 55 feet (?)

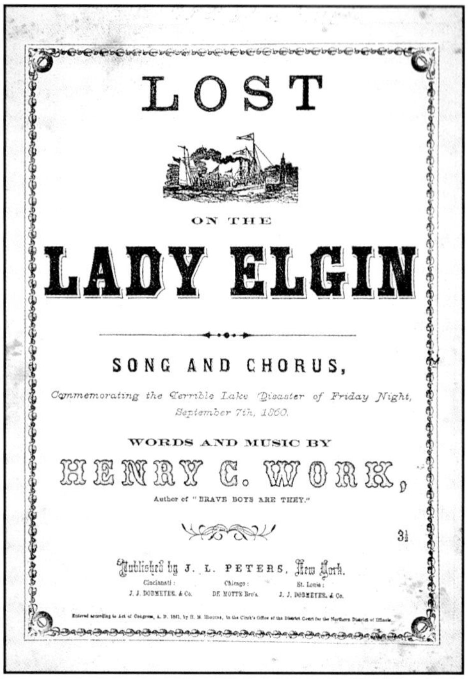

The number of people who died as a result the loss of the *Lady Elgin* was estimated to be somewhere between 279 and 298, thus ranking the event as one of the worst maritime disasters in Great Lakes history. The tragic circumstances fomented a profusion of editorials, memorials, dirges, and threnodies (such as the sheet music shown at right, from the author's collection). To put the catastrophe in perspective, the *Lady Elgin* was regarded in her time the way the *Edmund Fitzgerald* is regarded today.

The collision between the *Lady Elgin* and the schooner *Augusta* was featured in *Frank Leslie's Illustrated Newspaper*. In the woodcut at left, the artist used some artistic license in order to depict the fatal moment.

The hull soon broke apart. The largest section, containing the propulsion machinery, sank almost immediately. The deck separated from the hull and drifted toward shore, breaking apart gradually and spilling people and freight along the way. Today, wreckage is spread over several square miles.

The woodcut at left shows wreckage and people coming ashore. The one at right shows people clinging to the floating pilot house.

Harry Zych discovered the *Lady Elgin* in the summer of 1989. Shortly thereafter, he offered to show the wreck to Paul Ehorn, Joyce Hayward, and me. I felt especially privileged, for Zych trusted practically no one with the knowledge of the location of the site. We shipped aboard Paul Ehorn's boat, the *Sea Quest*, with Zych giving directions.

Strictly speaking, we did not dive the wreck either that day or the next. Instead, we dived on a debris field that Zych said stretched for miles. The main section of the hull, which comprised the engine and the boilers, lay a couple of miles away.

Fine silt that was suspended in the shallow water reduced visibility to five or six feet - hardly photographic quality. Nevertheless, it was easy to see that the rock-laden bottom was littered with shipboard relics. By groping along the lakebed I found numerous flintlock rifles, chinaware in abundance, silver plates and bowls, large copper pots, ornate brass fixtures, horseshoes, the capstan (whose cover exhibited a clean green patina), and many other items.

ROTARIAN

1889 to 1931 September 28
146 feet in length
Wooden-hulled excursion steamer
Maximum depth is 75 feet

After a long career as an excursion steamer, the *Rotarian* was employed as a dockside dance hall and restaurant. She sank at her berth, was raised and towed to her present location, and was scuttled. Prohibition-era bottles litter the site - although some of the cleaner ones did not seem to be original. The highlight of this wreck is the antique box boiler.

WELLS BURT

1873 to 1893 February 2
201 feet in length
Wooden-hulled schooner
Maximum depth is 35 feet

Only the stern is broken on this otherwise intact hull. Above and left: outside and inside the forecastle. Deadeyes are chained together to prevent removal.

Upon returning from my dive on the *Wells Burt*, I exclaimed, "That was the best dive I've made all year!" Then, remembering that it was only June, I added, "And the best dive I expect to make." It was.

STRAITS OF MACKINAC

I will never understand how "Mackinac" came to be pronounced "Mackin*aw*," but it is and we are stuck with it. Visitors are warned to use the correct pronunciation or they will be corrected by the local inhabitants and branded as tourists. Furthermore, despite the plurality in the name, there is only one strait. The strait attains a depth of 300 feet.

The Mackinac Bridge spans the gap between the Thumb and the Upper Peninsula. Through this gap passes the outflow of Lake Michigan into Lake Huron. At the strait, both upbound and downbound vessels are pinched together like grains of sand squeezing through the constriction in an hourglass. Local weather patterns have conspired with the convergence of the shipping lanes to create a dangerous area to traverse. A local concentration of shipwrecks is the result.

See the map on page 34 for the location of the *Sandusky* in the Straits of Mackinac.

SANDUSKY

1848 to 1856 September 20
110 feet in length
Wooden-hulled brig
Maximum depth is 80 feet

The *Sandusky* is not only one of the oldest identified wrecks in the Great Lakes, it is also one of the most accessible. An intact hull and jibboom, a profusion of deadeyes, and a beautifully carved figurehead, combine to make this an absolutely fascinating wreck. The figurehead, described both as a scroll head and a ram's head, is an excellent work of craftsmanship. Unfortunately, the original figurehead that is depicted above has been removed and replaced by a replica.

NORTH CHANNEL

The North Channel is an alternative route for vessels plying a course between Lake Superior and the lower lakes. The shipping lane passes north of Manitoulin Island and connects with the Georgian Bay. See the map on page 48 for the location of the North Channel.

The *North Wind* was negotiating this narrow passage when she struck Robertson Rock. The accompanying photographs clearly show a wreck that abides in a remarkable state of preservation. The superstructure has collapsed, but the hull has retained its integrity, thereby providing the experienced penetration diver with a fascinating tour of the below-decks corridors and compartments. Divers are warned, however, that the silt in some areas is several feet thick, and stirs up easily.

The lakebed surrounding the wreck consists of soft clay that is covered with extremely fine silt, as shown in the photograph at upper left (with the salamander). The thick hawsers above appear solid, but in reality they are as soft and squeezable as bathroom tissue.

Left and below: Where paint no longer adorns the interior partitions, the grain in the wood is evident.

NORTH WIND

1888 to 1926 July 21
299 feet in length
Steel-hulled bulk freighter
Maximum depth is 130 feet

Top: The risers that compose the engine room skylight have most of their glass panes intact.
Middle: This radiator once provided warmth for crew members who used the sink for washing.
Above left: A burbot swimming out of a metal toilet tank that has a wooden facade.
Above right: The outer bulkhead was boxed in, or paneled, much like a wall in a house.

GEORGIAN BAY

My introduction to the great wrecks of the Great Lakes took place off Tobermory, which lies at the end of the Bruce Peninsula. The Bruce Peninsula provides the enclosure that creates the Georgian Bay. See the map on page 48 for the location of the bay.

At the time of my first lake dive, the surrounding waters were known as Fathom Five Provincial Park. The name has since been changed to Fathom Five National Marine Park. By any name, the shipwrecks that lie within the boundaries of the Park are undoubtedly the most popular wreck sites in Canada, and possibly in the entire Great Lakes. This is due more to promotion than to the visual attraction of the wrecks - although they certainly do not lack appeal. Over the course of a weekend, a diver can "go there, do that, and buy the tee shirt" from the local tourist bureau. I recommend Tobermory highly for those who want to learn what Great Lakes wreck-diving is all about.

The first time I dived in the Park was a cold weekend in May. When strong winds prevented the boat from leaving the dock, I donned my scuba gear and went for a solo plunge in Little Tub Harbor. To my surprise, the rocky bottom was crawling with crayfish. And the crayfish were not just crawling about aimlessly - they were copulating!

Neither the proximity of the macro frame nor the blinding flash of the strobe disturbed the intense concentration on their activities, so my camera caught many of them in the act. With cool scientific detachment (some might say with lurid voyeuristic resolve) I carefully observed the mating behavior of this northern freshwater crustacean.

When two crayfish met, one (which I chauvinistically assumed was the male) wrestled with the female until he was able to flip her over onto her back. The female offered resistance to this maneuver, but either she was not as physically strong as the male or else she faked her resistance as part of the ritual, for she soon submitted passively while the male crept on top of her.

Next, the male held the female in place by gripping the knuckles of her claws in his pinchers. Ostensibly, this was to prevent her from assaulting him as he performed his part of the ritual. After the male mounted the female, their abdomens and telsons came together (no pun intended). And so begat the next generation of crayfish.

I am not a biologist, and cannot distinguish a male crayfish from the female of the species. So the female may have been the aggressor. That would put an entirely different light on the matter.

ARABIA

1853 to 1884 October 4
131 feet in length
Wooden-hulled bark
Maximum depth is 110 feet

The anchor resides on the thick bulwark. Deadeyes abound, many of them still secured to the chainplates. Blocks hang by their hooks from the bulwarks or from the fallen masts. The wreck's highlight, however, is the helm, which lies on the lakebed off the starboard stern.

A propeller shaft coupling and the flywheel are shown above and at upper right. The wooden hull, shown at lower right, is open for study. Below, a diver is putting himself through the hoops.

The *City of Grand Rapids* and the *Sweepstakes* lie about one hundred feet apart, making it easy to swim under water from one wreck to the other, then back again.

It is probable that more people have seen these two wrecks than any other wreck in the world.

CITY OF GRAND RAPIDS

1879 to 1907 October 29
123 feet in length
Wooden-hulled steamer
Maximum depth is 15 feet

SWEEPSTAKES

1867 to 1885 August
119 feet in length
Wooden-hulled schooner
Maximum depth is 20 feet

Above and below, stem to stern: The load line marks retain their paint, the rudder post is clamped in its bracket.

The most photogenic (and most photographed) feature of the *Sweepstakes* is the windlass (above). The hull (right) is readily penetrable, but has been placed off limits to divers because of the fear that oxygen in exhaust bubbles was accelerating deterioration. The hull is collapsing so badly that Park officials have braced it with cables, to prevent the outer bulkheads from spreading apart.

Lake Huron is the centerpiece of three lakes that share a common surface level, over which maritime traffic can proceed for 900 miles without interruption: from Chicago in Lake Michigan to Buffalo in Lake Erie.

Geologically, the North Channel and the Georgian Bay are extensions of Lake Huron, separated only by intervening islands and peninsulas.

The deepest part of Lake Huron is 750 feet.

LAKE HURON

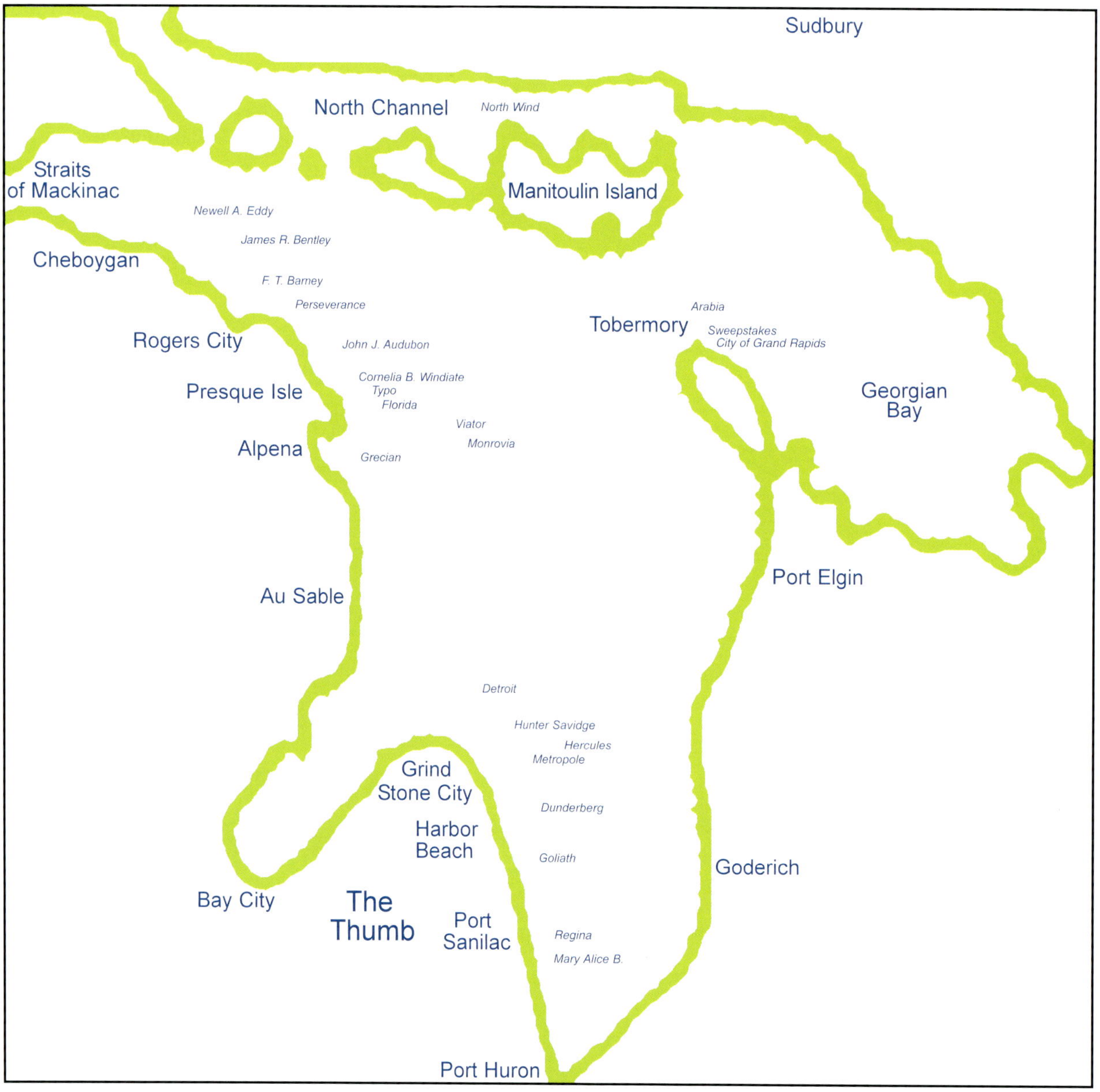

Left: Boaters need to keep a sharp lookout because many wrecks lie under the shipping lanes. A capable boat handler must be onboard at all times, to move the boat and avert getting run down by a vessel that is operating on autopilot.

Below and below left: Squalls appear quickly, sometimes passing through while divers are in the water, making it difficult to regain the boat.

Bottom: Many old lighthouses dot the shores. Most are no longer in operation except as tourist attractions. Left: Point Aux Barques. Right: Presque Isle.

The *Cornelia B. Windiate* lies in what I call "Schooner Alley" - a zone that extends along the coast northwest and southeast of Rogers City, between Bois Blanc Island and Presque Isle. I coined the name for the profusion of sailing vessels that litter the bottom like breadcrumbs in a canary cage. Judging by the number of shipwrecks that crowd this alley, it must have been a dangerous place for nineteenth-century mariners to negotiate. Fog, foul weather, and converging shipping lanes contributed to the many maritime casualties in this area.

Middle: Incredibly, the topsail yard is still secured to the foremast some fifty feet above the deck.
Above: The chainplates of the deadeyes are evident.
Left: The fife rail around the mast holds belaying pins. Note the spar and the sail hoops.

CORNELIA B. WINDIATE

1874 to 1875 November ?
138 feet in length
Wooden-hulled topsail schooner
Maximum depth is 180 feet

The date of this schooner's loss is unknown. She departed Milwaukee on November 28 - and was never seen again! The travel distance between her port of departure and her ultimate location is about 375 miles. Proceeding at 6 to 8 knots, she could have sailed that distance in two to three days.

This wreck's identity is not in doubt, as the images spread across the top of the preceding page and this one clearly show. The nameboard is so long that three photos were required to make all the letters readable.

Upper right: Kevin Magee hovers over the bulwark. Below: Lifeboat on the lakebed. Right: Hearteye.

CORNELIA B. WINDIATE

Continued

The *Cornelia B. Windiate* is small enough that you can see it all in a single dive. But you can't absorb everything that the wreck has to offer. You must dive it again . . . and again . . . and again . . .

The after cabin is intact. Shown above is the curving staircase that leads to the after deck. The interior is shown at upper left: a standing door, part of a table, a stool, separating partitions, and a deep layer of fine silt.

Above: Some of the running rigging fell onto the cabin roof and across the narrow promenade. Most of the white specks are zebra mussels.

Right: The outside after wall of the cabin, showing the stovepipe opening and two windows, one with bars. Most of the white specks are dabs of paint on the nail heads.

Left: The foremast rises more than 60 feet above the deck. Adhering to a safe rate of ascent of 30 feet per minute, it took me two full minutes to ascend from the deck to the mooring chain at the top of the mast.

Below: The wooden helm appears to have been dislodged from its proper position by a fallen mast.

Bottom left: A spider's web of running rigging lies atop the hatch cover, which is still secured by strongbacks.

Bottom right: A view of the fantail, showing a porthole opening and a decorative iron star. The impression of another star is visible to the left. The horizontal white streaks are caulking between the planks.

Somebody once told me that early marine engines were built of wood. I scoffed at the notion, noting the impossibility of containing steam in a wooden cylinder with a wooden piston. A little research revealed that, while the pistons and cylinders were made of iron, the supporting structure was indeed made of wood. But I never saw such an engine until I dived on the *Detroit*.

The *Detroit's* engine consists of a massive pyramidal structure that towers thirty feet or more above the main deck. The geometry of the frame is more like that of the Eiffel Tower than the pyramids of Egypt: tall and slender rather than squat. The framework is skeletal, also like the Eiffel Tower. The corner supports are made from timbers so thick that they put railroad ties to shame. The four corners converge on a platform near the top, then continue upward to where they are secured together. The wooden platform holds in place the iron sleeve of the piston rod, which reciprocates vertically. The iron cylinder is located at the level of the deck. Most of the deck is intact.

Top left: A wooden paddle blade.
Middle left: The paddle blade supports converge near the hub.
Bottom left: The hub, from which the paddle blade supports extend.
Below: the paddle wheel boxes are gone, but the paddle wheel frames and the paddle blades are still in place.

Opposite page, bottom left: Mounted on the boiler is a sight tube, whose glass is unbroken. In the background, the green painted wood is the facade on the engine cylinder.
Opposite page, bottom right: This copper sighting ball is mounted on the tip of the bowsprit. It acted as a sighting device, like the range finder on the end of a gun barrel.

DETROIT

1846 to 1854 May 25
157 feet in length
Wooden-hulled sidewheel steamer
Maximum depth is 180 feet

The most astonishing feature of the sidewheeler *Detroit* is the large bronze bell and its unusual placement: inside the engine support structure, between the apex and the piston platform. After photographing the bell from both sides and from a variety of angles, I rapped the clanger against the inside. The resulting ring was clear but possessed a pitch that was lower than normal - as if the vibrations were somehow altered by the density of the water, or muted by the rubber material pressed against my ears.

"NOVELTY WORKS" was embossed on one side of the bell. "NEW YORK 1844" was embossed on the other side. The instant I read the embossing I thought of John Ericsson's *Monitor*, the Civil War ironclad, which was launched in 1862. The Novelty Iron Works built the *Monitor's* turret.

Unfortunately, visibility rarely exceeds half a dozen feet.

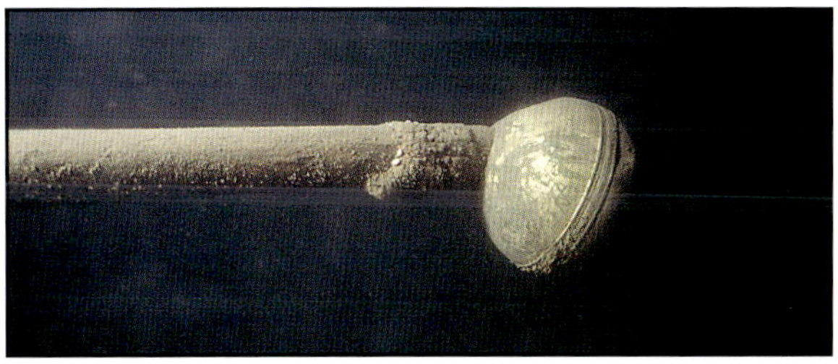

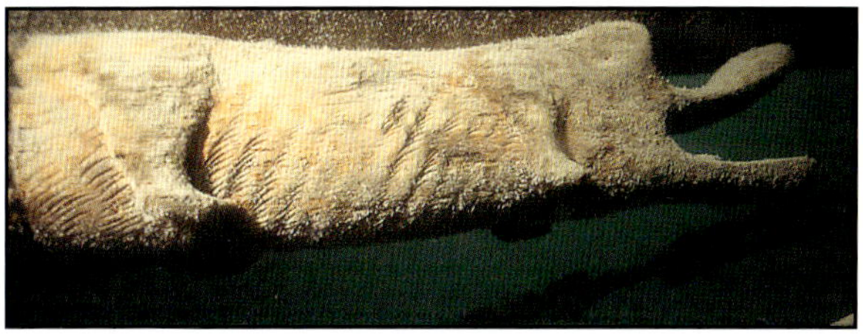

DUNDERBERG

1867 to 1868 August 13
186 feet in length
Wooden-hulled schooner
Maximum depth is 155 feet

Opposite top: Note the red dot of paint in the eye.
Opposite left and right: Detail of the trailboard's artistry.
Top: I took the left photo in 1988, the right one in 1999. Note that the testicles are no longer evident. (As a biological side note, reptiles do not exhibit external genitalia.)
Below: The Roman numerals are load line numbers on the stem. The chains loop in a catenary past the figurehead to the end of the bowsprit.
Bottom right: The fancy carving on the underneath of the cathead.

When I first dived the *Dunderberg*, I proclaimed that it was one of the top five shipwrecks that I had ever seen. Since that time I have expanded my list to ten, but I still count the *Dunderberg* among the top five. The reason for my enthusiasm was the wreck's primary attraction: the beautifully carved, stylized alligator figurehead, and the intricately ornate trailboards that grace both bows (port and starboard).

I was so enthralled by the *Dunderberg* that I was moved to research the circumstances of her loss (by collision), and write an article about my mind-blowing dive. After magazine publication, I included the article in my book, *Wreck Diving Adventures*.

FLORIDA

1889 to 1897 May 20
271 feet in length
Wooden-hulled package freighter
Maximum depth is 195 feet

After a long career in wreck-diving, it is rare for a newly-dived shipwreck to excite me as much as I was excited by the *Florida*. I was so enthralled by this vintage freighter that I instantly added it to my list of favorite wrecks: one of my top ten.

The hull is intact except for the collision hole, which extends through two decks in the midship cargo hold, and the demolished engine room. The railing is contiguous for nearly the entire length of the upper deck. The hull is constructed of wood, but the stem is protected by a metal shield on which the load line numerals are scratched.

Shown above is the peripatetic capstan cover. I first found it secreted between the starboard bow bulwark and a displaced ventilator. By the end of the week, helpful divers had moved it to its original position atop the capstan (right top and bottom). The central green splotch is the result of corrosion.

Above: Reverse lettering on the inside of the hull. Note the tie-down fitting at lower left.
Below: A barrel expanded by the swelling of its contents, and a coil of rope.
Bottom: A handling cart or dolly.

Packaged freight stowed in the cargo holds. Top: Stacked wash basins. Above: Tubs and wash basins perched atop tiered metal containers. Below: A pail and wash basins.

FLORIDA

Continued

Right: These airtight cans were imploded by pressure at depth.
Below: Three walls of the main deck cabin remain standing. This fire axe is mounted on the outside of the forward wall.

Lanterns were stowed on the starboard side of the main deck cabin (below left), along with extra glass globes (above right). A thoughtful diver placed one lantern outside for display (below right).

The cabin abaft the main deck cabin covers the top of the boiler, which is so large that it protrudes above the upper deck.

Above: A boiler gauge placed on the after deck by a considerate diver.

Above left: These glass sight tubes indicated the water level in the boiler.

The engine room bulkheads have collapsed, exposing the propulsion machinery.

Above: A gauge panel secured to the starboard side of the engine.

Above right: The after capstan cover is identical to the one on the bow. A diver found this one under debris, and placed it atop an engine cylinder for easy viewing.

Right: The bell lies in the debris field to port.

F. T. BARNEY

1856 to 1868 October 23
130 feet in length
Wooden-hulled schooner
Maximum depth is 160 feet

Like the *Cornelia B. Windiate*, the *F. T. Barney* lies in "Schooner Alley." Upright and intact, the wreck affords an excellent opportunity to study the construction and rigging of a nineteenth-century sailing vessel.

Left: A hearteye hangs from the end of the bowsprit. The base of the jibboom is visible above.

Below left: This wood stock anchor hangs precariously by the edge of a fluke.

Below: The anchor's ringbolt is drawn up to the cathead and is secured by a short length of chain.

Right: A block hanging by a chain through a hole in the bulwark. Note the shadow of the hook.

Left: A two-sheave block rests on the lakebed at the base of the stem.

Above: The top of the bulwark is crowded with deadeyes, blocks, and a belaying pin. Note the fallen spars in the background.
Top right: A shovel leaning against a pile of anchor chain, abaft the after bulkhead of the forecastle.
Right: A hatch cover still in place.
Below: A hearteye hanging off the bow. The stem is visible at left.
Bottom right: This lantern is resting on the lakebed along with several loose planks.

F. T. BARNEY

Continued

All but the forward wall of the deck cabin is intact. The ambient light photo at left is looking aft from atop the roof. The compass dominates the foreground, while the helm is shown in the background.

Below left: The helm (looking forward).
Below right: The compass perched atop its storage cabinet, on the after wall of the cabin.
Bottom left: A ceramic bowl and a pair of deadeyes, in front of the missing forward wall.
Bottom right: Ceramic plates and bowls are nearly buried by fine silt inside the cabin.

GOLIATH

1846 to 1851 November 3
131 feet in length
Wooden-hulled freighter
Maximum depth is 100 feet

Commonly poor visibility presents a challenge to the photographer. My fascination with this wreck, however, does not reside with its photographic potential, but with its historic significance. The *Goliath's* propulsion machinery was the brainchild of inventor John Ericsson, the erratic genius who designed and built the Civil War ironclad *Monitor*. That association alone is enough to imbue this wreck with strong personal interest, due to my long-time battle with the bureaucracy at NOAA that sought (unsuccessfully) to prevent me from diving the *Monitor*.

The *Goliath* was a bad luck vessel. Archival records are contradictory. According to one document, she exploded on September 19, 1848 off Goderich, Ontario (on the east coast of Lake Huron), with the loss of 22 lives. According to another, she blew up on September 20, 1848 at Point aux Barques, Michigan (on the west coast of Lake Huron), with the loss of 18 lives.

Either she did not sink at that time or she was salvaged, for ultimately she stranded on November 3, 1851 off Thunder Bay, Michigan, with no loss of life.

One special engineering feature of the *Goliath* was the advanced twin-screw design. Both propellers were counter-rotated by one single-piston engine, by means of a pair of offset shafts that were geared to vertical connecting rod assemblies.

Another innovative feature was the Ericsson propeller, shown at left and above, but seen more clearly at right (with Joyce Hayward). This mechanical marvel was actually two propellers and a Kort nozzle in one: three interior blades that were fastened to the inside of a shroud to which six exterior blades were riveted in alternation with the interior blades.

GRECIAN

1891 to 1906 June 7
296 feet in length
Steel-hulled bulk freighter
Maximum depth is 100 feet

The *Grecian* is broken in two. The sections are connected by a long debris field that is difficult to follow. As a result, moorings have been established at either end: to the windlass on the bow, to the tiller arm on the stern. Because the after section contains the engine room and general quarters, it is more interesting to explore than the bow section - although the bow section is not without its merit.

Top left: The mooring line on the windlass.
Left, second from top: A double mooring bitt.
Above left: The capacious cargo hold.
Left: Wooden railing.
Above right: Lifeboat davit.

Above: The mooring line secured to the tiller arm. Note the curved taffrail in the background.
Top right: Flag pole holder above the centerline scupper.
Right: The triple-expansion reciprocating steam engine is exposed, permitting easy access to interior compartments.
Bottom right: Glass sight tube on the engine room bulkhead.
Below: Steering cable running over a pulley wheel.

GRECIAN

Continued

Top left: Not a typical oiler, but what appears to be a multiple oil-feed station.
Top right: Bench vice.
Left: Throttle controls for the engine.
Bottom left: Zebra mussels clustered on the lip of a porcelain sink.
Below: Fuse box.

Above: A bathtub filled with boards and silt.
Top right: A porcelain toilet.
Right: Divers exploring the interior must be careful not to stir up silt, and of becoming entangled in cables. Always carry a back-up light.
Below: The bottom blade of the propeller is broken off at the base.
Bottom right: A close-up view of the two remaining blades. Note the rusticles and zebra mussels.

HERCULES

1904 to 1932 December 23
115 feet in length
Wooden-hulled dredge
Maximum depth is 190 feet

The *Hercules* is only for the hardy - those who are willing to grope about a deep wreck in body-length visibility. I recommend that divers be proficient in their use of a line reel, or confident in their ability in underwater orienteering. Despite cold water and poor diving conditions, the wreck possesses some distinctive features that make it worthwhile to explore: primarily the huge cage-like derrick, but also the hoisting tackle - thick steel cables and massive pulleys.

The *Hercules* is a barge on which a tall crane is mounted (upper left). The wooden hull is so spanking clean in places that the planks still show their grain. (above). The iron mooring bitts are badly oxidized, yet the ropes that wrap around them or stretch across the deck are nicely preserved (left and bottom left). Brass gauges appear to be part of a welding outfit (below).

HUNTER SAVIDGE

1879 to 1899 August 20
117 feet in length
Wooden-hulled schooner
Maximum depth is 150 feet

For such a small wreck, the *Hunter Savidge* displays a fair amount of rigging. Standing rigging - such as blocks, deadeyes, and belaying pins - grace the bulwarks (above right). Many of the deadeyes that comprise the running rigging lie on the granular lakebed (right). The aluminum drink cans are of recent vintage. However, the china cup shown below is contemporary with the wreck. At below right, a fallen mast is still ringed with sail hoops.

JAMES R. BENTLEY

1867 to 1878 November 12
178 feet in length
Wooden-hulled schooner
Maximum depth is 160 feet

This is another "Schooner Alley" wreck, like the *Cornelia B. Windiate*, but not nearly as intact. The top point of the bow is broken off (above) just forward of the hawsepipe. A hearteye adorns the wooden hull (top right), and belaying pins rest like dowels in holes along the inboard side of the bulwark (middle right). Fishing nets lie draped across the upper deck, as shown below: snagged on a mooring bitt (left) and covering a pail (right).

The cabin has collapsed, yet some of its ornateness is still evident, as in the carved block work in the top right photo. Several glass windows and frames survived the breakdown, as shown below and at right. Above, a pottery shard lies on the silt-covered deck.

Bottom left: Load line marks on the rudder post.
Below: Deadeye and bull's-eye on the outboard rail.

JOHN J. AUDUBON

1854 to 1854 October 20
About 110 feet in length
Wooden-hulled brig
Maximum depth is 165 feet

The *John J. Audubon* lies in "Schooner Alley," along with the *Cornelia B. Windiate* and other fine sailing vessels of yesteryear.

This wreck is almost too good to be true: an intact museum piece that has lain undisturbed for a century and a half. The only major evidence of deterioration is the broken masts. The photo above shows from a distance the manner in which masts were stepped. At left is a close-up shown from beneath the step.

Above: Anchor chain leading through a deck flange into the chain locker. A corner of the chain locker hatch is in view.

Far left: A ceramic container sitting next to the windlass drum.

Left: Centerline deck supports inside the hold. The notches cut into the near support functioned as ladder rungs.

The standing mast shown at top left is fitted with a fife rail, or spider band. Not only are the belaying pins still in place, but one is doing the duty for which it was designed.

The top right photo shows broken spars, wire rigging, a single-sheave block, and a pair of two-sheave blocks - lying on a thickly silted deck.

Shown above is a distant view of the helm, where it came to rest against the after starboard bulwark. Note the wooden box in the foreground. At right is a close-up view of the helm.

JOHN J. AUDUBON

Continued

Top left: An intact earthenware jar, broken crockery, and a plate.

Left: At first glance, the red spar appears to be painted wood. The giveaway, however, is the presence of lumps of iron oxide that are produced by iron-reducing bacteria. The carmine stain is rust. Note the bucket with the bale and the large chunks of coal. The coal was undoubtedly burned in the cook stove.

Bottom left: The tiller arm. Note the large block on the inside ledge of the fantail, and the white china pitcher under the ledge.

Below: A close-up of the pitcher.

MARY ALICE B.

1931 to 1975 September 5
62 feet in length
Steel-hulled tug
Maximum depth is 90 feet

This cute and accessible little tug offers odd items of interest. There is no doubt about the wreck's identity - the name is stencilled on both sides of the bow. The handsomely crafted wooden wheel beckons a helmsman to grab the handles and steer a course for port. The bronze helm stand is securely bolted to the deck.

METROPOLE

1883 to 1903 August 8
118 feet in length
Wooden-hulled bulk freighter
Maximum depth is 160 feet

Despite fine silt that blankets the wreck and hangs in suspension, the *Metropole* is an unforgettable site: a definite "must see."

Above: To "head" off this photo section is a single seater.

Left: The engine cylinder is planked with a wood facade.

Far left: A sight glass mounted above the engine cylinder.

Below: Steam whistle.
Bottom right: A glass kerosene lantern lying within the curl of a rope.

I was appalled when I first dived the wreck and found initials painted on the companionway bulkhead. I jumped to the conclusion that the initials were those of the divers who had discovered the wreck. I was wrong! They were the initials of former crew members.

In the after cabin, both port and starboard companionways held wooden spools of carefully wound fire hose.

Most of the loose china came to rest against the port bulkhead, implying that the ship rolled to port in the process of sinking, then settled upright on the bottom. I still wonder what might be inside the wooden box on the top shelf of the cabinet.

METROPOLE

Continued

Top right: Cabin window with unbroken pane.
Above and right: Galley items.
Below and bottom right: The helm inside the wheel house. Spinning the helm either wound or unwound the wire rope on the shaft: actions that swung the rudder.

MONROVIA

1943 to 1959 June 25
447 feet in length
Steel-hulled freighter
Maximum depth is 140 feet

Local lore has it that the *Monrovia* was a Liberty ship. Although she has the appearance of one, she is not. Liberty ships were built in U.S. shipyards according to a standard design. The *Monrovia* was built in England. By any standard, however, this is a huge wreck to explore. Do not expect to see it all in a single dive.

At the time of her loss, the *Monrovia* was registered in Monrovia. This accounts for the double display of the word on the curved fantail.

Above: A vaulting, double-deck compartment above the machinery spaces.

Right: Electrical panel in the engine room.

I call this "Dali's melting porthole" after the melting clocks in Salvadore Dali's surrealistic paintings. Although the hull is contiguous there are places where damage is considerable and where stress has caused deformtion.

MONROVIA

Continued

Top left: The bars in the windows make this deck house seem like a prison.
Beneath top left: Inset paneling.
Above: Note the rusticles on the back of the stove.

Above: There is something fishy about this photo. Note the ears and outline of the porthole lying in the silt.
Right: A close-up view of the wooden cabinet. The glass pane in the left door is unbroken.

At left, my exhaust bubbles are escaping from the skylight above the machinery spaces long after my exit. Access to the interior is deceptively simple. Catwalks encircling the engine sometimes lead to dead ends that are out of sight of the overhead entrance.

Above left: The cables beyond this fallen door are a hazard.
Above: A dish amid collapsed partitions.
Left: The paint locker.

I was befuddled by this object shown at right. I am still befuddled. It appears to be the solidified remains of a substance that was carried in a barrel.

The *Newell A. Eddy* is unmistakably identifiable. Her name is split onto two nameboards that grace her bows. As shown in the top two photos, "Newell" is printed on the starboard bow, "A. Eddy" on the port bow. The close-up at left shows detail of the fancy curlicues that bracket the lettering.

This is another wreck that lies in "Schooner Alley." Both the *Newell A. Eddy* and the *Cornelia B. Windiate* sport standing foremasts that tower more than sixty feet above the deck, each with a mooring line secured to the top. This created a logbook conundrum: should the two minutes required to climb the mast count as bottom time or ascent time? For decompression purposes, I opted to count it as ascent time.

Note the sail hoops and fife rail on the mast below, and the load marks on the stem at left.

NEWELL A. EDDY

1890 to 1893 April 20
242 feet in length
Wooden-hulled schooner
Maximum depth is 160 feet

Should one overlook the nameboards, another way to establish the identity of the *Newell A. Eddy* is to read the lettering on the brass capstan cover. The date of construction as well as the name and place of the capstan's manufacturer are also stamped on the cover. Kevin Magee is pictured above.

Below left and right: Note the subtle differences in the cathead arrangements. The port cathead is fitted with a hearteye, while the starboard one is fitted with a deadeye.

PERSEVERANCE

1855 to 1864 November 24
121 feet in length
Wooden-hulled schooner
Maximum depth is 130 feet

Except for the forward section, the hull of the *Perseverance* is considerably broken down, yet the wreck possesses some salient points of interest.

I cannot state positively that the carving mounted to the top of the cutwater (left) is a figurehead, or even a scroll head, but the finial is definitely ornamental.

Above is a bull's eye.

The panoramic view at bottom left shows range, while the close-up view below adds detail.

The general state of deterioration can be seen in the photo above. At top right is a globular ceramic jug complete with lettering under the glaze. A brown globular jug is shown at right.

Below, wooden shovel handles lie haphazardly in the debris.

Miscellaneous items, such as the copper bowl and the ceramic jar shown at bottom right, are found largely in the after section.

REGINA

1907 to 1913 November 10-13
249 feet in length
Steel-hulled freighter
Maximum depth is 80 feet

The *Regina* foundered in the notorious Great Lakes Storm of November 1913. The tempest howled for four consecutive days. During that time a dozen vessels sank, more than a score suffered damage, and some 250 people died. The precise date of the *Regina's* loss is unknown: she disappeared without a trace and none of her crew members survived.

The archival photo printed above evokes the awful tragedy of that storm. The bodies of these drowned sailors washed up on a deserted strand, but most disappeared without a trace.

It is important to remember that the shipwrecks that we dive today for fun and recreation, are but wood or iron remnants of misfortunes of the past.

Above: A dramatic view looking up at the propeller and rudder.
Bottom left: The name on the fantail.
Below: Porthole in cramped quarters.

The zebra mussel infestation is a double-edged sword. On one edge the visibility has improved spectacularly, while on the other edge the shells have covered the wrecks to an incredible degree.

Note the change in the lettering on the port bow. I took the top left photo in 1992, and the top right photo in 2000. The brass letters are now exposed only because considerate divers continually scrape the mussel shells off of them.

Right: Even this ladder inside the cargo hold is thickly encrusted with zebra mussels.

The *Regina* is a fascinating wreck to explore. A diver can enter the hull at the stern from underneath, pass the electrical panel shown at bottom left, swim under the engine and boiler depicted below, and exit from the forward cargo hold.

TYPO

1873 to 1899 October 14
137 feet in length
Wooden-hulled schooner
Maximum depth is 185 feet

Not another one in "Schooner Alley"? Yes, I am afraid so. Unlike the incomparable *Cornelia B. Windiate*, the *Typo* is considerably broken apart. But no wreck having a bell still mounted on its davit can be entirely devoid of interest, even if the bell is made of iron. As the reader can see, the surface of the bell is rusted, covered with silt, and sprinkled with zebra mussels. If any lettering exists under this obfuscatory pall, I was unable to determine if there were any misspellings.

Below: Two hearteyes are secured to the starboard cathead. The vertical timber in the background is the anchor stock.

Bottom right: Fallen booms and topmasts litter the wreck like pick-up sticks (a pre-computer game for children).

VIATOR

1904 to 1935 October 31
231 feet in length
Steel-hulled freighter
Maximum depth is 175 feet

Although visibility on the *Viator* ranges from bad to awful, the exploratory potential is vast. The steering engine at left, located in the wheel house, is the size of a printing press. The surrounding photos show the interior: ornate woodwork in the process of collapse.

VIATOR

Continued

Top left: The steel hull is heavily "rusticled."
Left: The lantern closet, loaded with spares.
Above: A lantern with a bulb but no lens.
Bottom left: This Norwegian freighter has cans from Oslo.
Bottom right: White caulking between strips of paneling.

LAKE ERIE

With a maximum depth of 210 feet, Lake Erie is the shallowest of the Great Lakes.

After my first dive in Lake Erie, in 1989, I vowed never again to return. Visibility was only three feet. I kept that promise for ten years. When I next dived in Lake Erie, in 1999, visibility had increased to seventy-five feet. I was so enthralled that I repealed my vow. So what caused the improvement?

My first dive was at the western end of the lake, where visibility is still poor. Visibility is far superior at the eastern end.

The other cause was the recent invasion of zebra mussels: bivalve mollusks that were supposedly transported from Europe in the ballast tanks of transatlantic "salties."

Zebra mussels are both a curse and a blessing - largely the former. Their shells clog water intakes and blanket shipwrecks. But because they are filter feeders, they have vacuumed much of the nutrients and sediment out of the water, thus increasing the clarity.

At right, the interior of the *Carlingford* is a prime example.

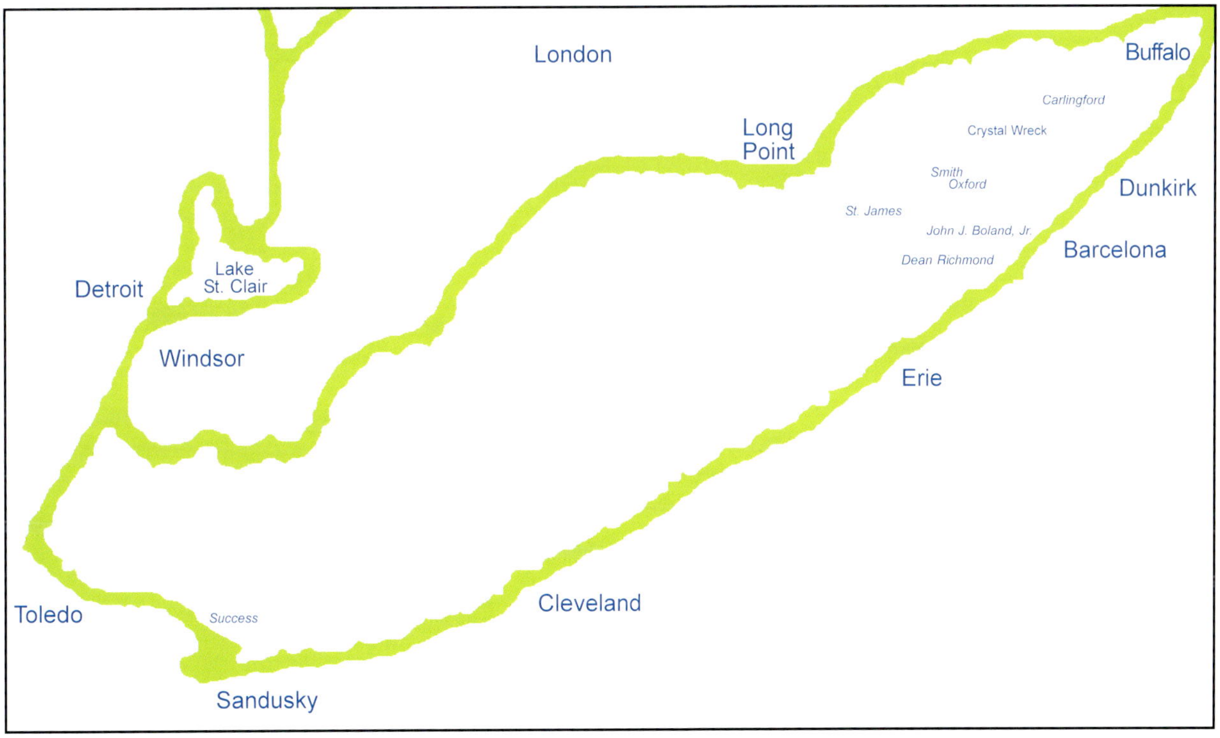

Although the hull of this schooner is largely intact, the masts are conspicuously missing. The spider ring (above) is unbroken, giving me pause to wonder how the mast was removed without causing damage.

CARLINGFORD

1869 to 1881 November 12
130 feet in length
Wooden-hulled schooner
Maximum depth is 95 feet

Top left: The shapes that delineate the deadeyes and chainplates are barely discernible beneath multiple layers of zebra mussels.
Above: The cargo hold is open and accessible. Note the hanging knees that support the deck.
Above right: Close-up of a hanging knee.
Right: This anchor lies off the port bow.

CRYSTAL WRECK

Unidentified
About 130 feet in length
Wooden-hulled sailing vessel
Maximum depth is 120 feet

The Crystal Wreck is representative of the trade-off between clarity and obscurity. Overall visibility is stunning, but specific objects such as deadeyes (below) appear formless and nondescript. The shape of the pump at bottom left is more distinct.

The mooring line is secured to the port bow where a twisted fishing net is snagged (left and far left).

DEAN RICHMOND

1864 to 1893 August 14
238 feet in length
Wooden-hulled freighter
Maximum depth is 110 feet

The greenish silhouette of the propeller (above) gives little indication of the zebra mussels that blanket the blades and hull (right).

Below: A burbot swims past the mussel-encrusted lower hull.

Bottom right: Over the years, the wreck has settled into the clay of which the lakebed is comprised.

JOHN J. BOLAND, JR.

1928 to 1932 October 5
252 feet in length
Steel-hulled freighter
Maximum depth is 130 feet

Top left: The propeller in silhouette.
Above: The exterior of the hull is blanketed with zebra mussels, obscuring most details.
Left: Zebra mussels have even invaded the interior. Given a choice of substrate, they seem to prefer caulking to wood.
Bottom left: A diver cruising over the railing.
Below: The wreck lies nearly upside down, as shown by this view of the promenade deck.

Until this site was identified, the *Oxford* was called the Tiller Wreck or Crow's-Nest Wreck, after those two distinctive features (above and top right). Although clear patches exist, most of the wreck is thickly encrusted with zebra mussels. The cleats and the lower mast at right are completely encrusted. The face of one deadeye below is clear. At bottom right, zebra mussels have inexplicably avoided a swath on the hull. Note the caulking between planks.

OXFORD

1842 to 1856 May 30
114 feet in length
Wooden-hulled brig
Maximum depth is 165 feet

Top left: Deadeyes and belaying pins are cemented to the bulwark by zebra mussels.

Top right: The shape of this deadeye is nearly obscured by encrustation.

Above: Oddly, this scroll head lying on the silty lakebed is practically free of zebra mussels.

Left: Zebra mussels have invaded the interior. Note the hanging knee that supports the deck.

SMITH

1881 to 1930 October 25
120 feet in length
Wooden-hulled tug
Maximum depth is 160 feet

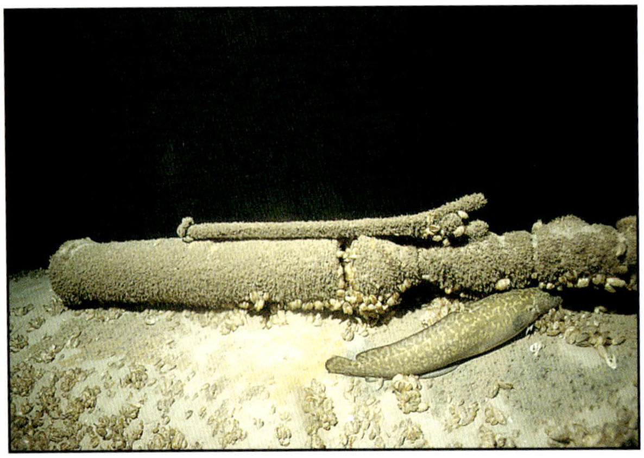

The hull and wheel house of this old wooden tug are largely intact. Rich nutrients flow through the open wheel house to support a vigorous colony of zebra mussels. Nonetheless, the helm (upper right) and telegraph (right) remain relatively free from encrustation, as does the steam whistle on the lakebed (above, with burbot).

At left is a cluster of zebra mussels living on a lump of coal. The close-up at bottom right focuses on a single individual. The conundrum that continues to plague scientists is: Are the shells of zebra mussels colored white with black stripes, or black with white stripes?

ST. JAMES

1856 to 1870 October ?
118 feet in length
Wooden-hulled schooner
Maximum depth is 165 feet

(Previously known as Schooner X.)

Casual observation of the figurehead might not reveal differences that were caught by the camera. Not only is the starboard face nearly free of growth, but each face is carved somewhat differently.

Bottom left: The wooden helm is more than half buried in fine powdery silt.

Below: Not only is this mast standing tall, but some of the wire rigging trails from the truck.

SUCCESS

1790 (or 1840) to 1946 July 4
135 feet in length
Wooden-hulled barkentine
Maximum depth is 15 feet

The reader might wonder why I included a wreck for which I have no underwater photos. The *Success* is here not because of stunning visual appeal but because of its age and historic interest.

According to the publications shown below, the *Success* was launched in 1790 as a convict ship, and for decades was occupied in the transportation of felons from England to Australia. After a long and varied career, she ended her days as a barkentine museum piece that displayed the laurels of her infamous past: prison cells, hobbling devices, torture contraptions, and so on. How much of this reconstructed memoir was hype for the public is often questioned. Some people even doubt her advertised launching date, claiming instead that the *Success* was not built until 1840.

Be that as it may, in the first half of the twentieth century the *Success* was exhibited in England, New York, and the Great Lakes. Untold millions of people toured her throughout the years.

I have no underwater photos because when I dived the wreck, visibility was less than one foot - and I was told that bad viz was typical. I groped along the bottom like a mole, feeling rather than seeing wooden planks. But I felt some satisfaction at having touched this historic site.

All the items shown on this page are in the author's personal collection.

The brochure at left, those at bottom left, and the books at bottom right, all tout the antiquity of the *Success*.

Despite differences in the titles, the books are little more than slight variations of the same, with some minor revisions in the text. Numerous editions exist.

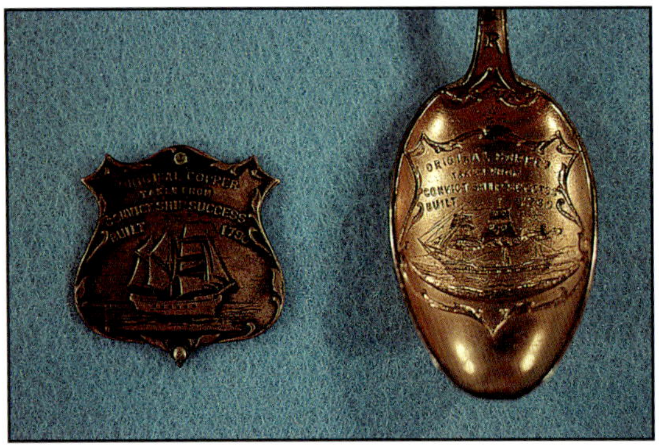

Souvenir items, like these shown at left and right, can occasionally be found on the collector's market.

LAKE ONTARIO

The south and west coasts of Lake Ontario are rather citified. But much of the northern lakeside, particularly in the northeast quadrant, is largely free from the blight of civilization. Wilderness and wild shores abound. Maximum depth is 800 feet.

Above: Beaver-chewed tree.

Right: An isolated strand.

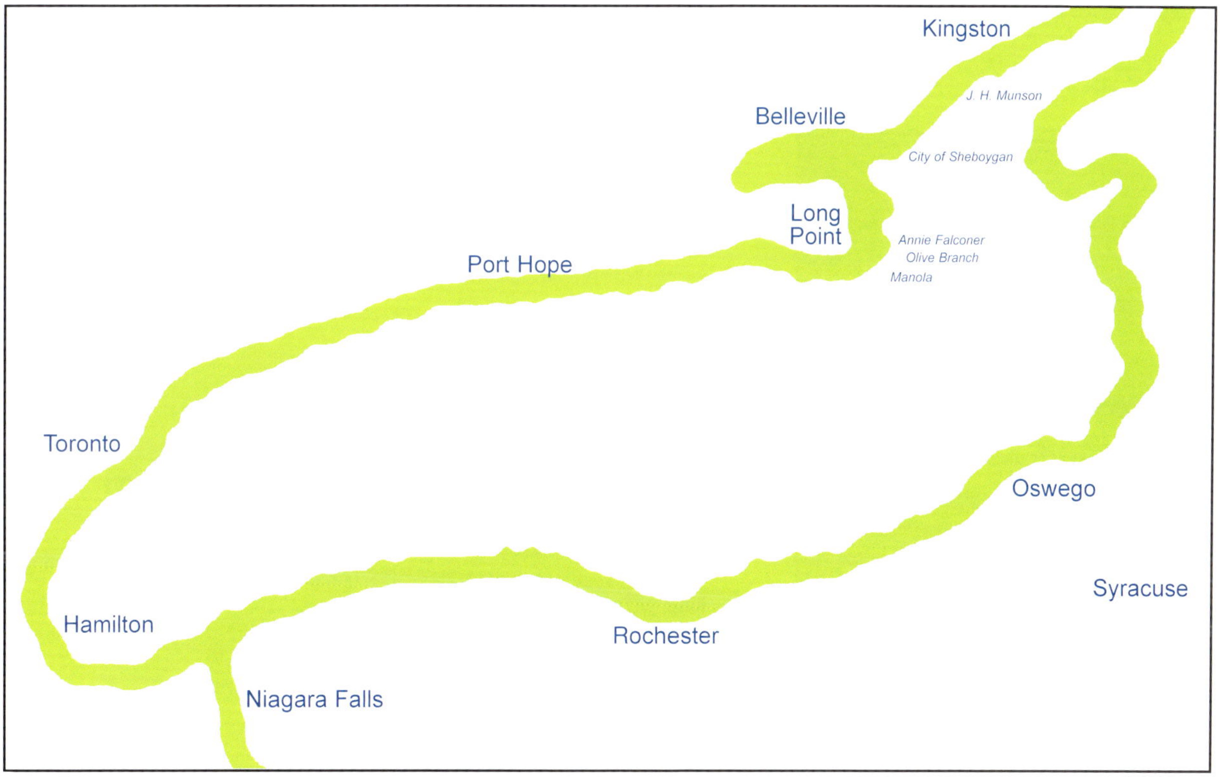

ANNIE FALCONER

1867 to 1904 November 12
108 feet in length
wooden-hulled schooner
Maximum depth is 80 feet

The word for this wreck is "cute" - or perhaps "petite." It is small enough to circumnavigate slowly several times, in order to absorb all the features that it has to present.

Top left and right: The wooden helm and a precariously perched anchor. Above: Deadeyes and wire rigging atop the bulwark. Left: An eel glides up along the hull and bulwark. Below: A fish carcass resting on the muddy bottom.

CITY OF SHEBOYGAN

1871 to 1915 September 25
135 feet in length
Wooden-hulled schooner
Maximum depth is 100 feet

The *City of Sheboygan* is a "gotta see" wreck - and one dive is not nearly enough. There is plenty of ambient light and the visibility is generally spectacular.

Above left and right: The bowsprit is broken off but some of the deck planks still cover the forecastle and support the capstan.

Right: A mast platform lies edgewise on the intact deck, along with some of the rigging.

Below left: Windlass and anchor chain.

Below right: Anchor chain and hawsepipe.

Above: The glass sight tube on the donkey boiler is unbroken.
Top right: A lifeboat davit swings over the starboard stern quarter. Note the block, the caulking between planks, the open hatch, the kitchen ware near the samson post, and the zebra mussels.
Right: A perfect example of a maststep.
Below (from inboard looking outboard): Belaying pins stowed in the pinrail.
Bottom right (from outboard looking inboard): A good view of the chainplates that hold the deadeyes.

CITY OF SHEBOYGAN

Continued

Above left: The smooth rectangular inlay in the plank is a deck prism. Shown above is the same deck prism seen from underneath.

Left: Wooden blocks and wire tackle literally litter the deck.

Bottom left: A cast iron stove.

Below: The exposed portion of the rudder. The block would have been secured to a cleat on the fantail by means of a stout line. The assembly would save the rudder from becoming lost if it was accidentally unshipped.

J. H. MUNSON

? to 1890 April 3
About 75 feet in length
Wooden-hulled dredge
Maximum depth is 115 feet

Most divers would not get excited at the prospect of diving a common dredge. But the *J.H. Munson* is an exception to the rule, and makes for an exceptional dive. The thick timbers of the hull are in excellent condition. The top deck hangs like a roof over a pavilion. There is a great deal to see inside (under the deck).

Top left: A stout wooden samson post.
Top middle: An intact glass sight tube on the boiler.
Top right: A workbench complete with tools and vice.

Above: This pressure gauge faceplate is clearly legible.
Right: Dredge crews had to eat on the job. Here is proof!

MANOLA

1890 to 1918 December 3
282 feet in length
Steel-hulled bulk freighter
Maximum depth is 80 feet

The *Manola* is actually half a wreck - but a half that is well worth exploring. After being cut in two in order to fit through the Welland Canal, the forward section foundered in a storm. It came to rest upside down. The forecastle deck holds the hull partly off the bottom. This allows access to the cargo hold and the forward compartments - and to the nautical relics that abide there.

Top right: A loose porthole that is lying outside the wreck.

Right, second from top: An outside view of a porthole in the forecastle bulwark. My strobe light was reflected off the glass. The rust behind the glass is on the inside of the storm cover.

Right, third from top: The same porthole seen from inside.

Bottom left: Extension lights.

Bottom right: A navigational lantern with a Fresnel lens.

MANOLA

Continued

The hold is vast and without major landmarks, and some compartments in the forecastle are laden with silt. Divers should be cautious when penetrating the wreck.

The cage lamps shown in the left column appear to be bolted to the deck instead of to the overhead. The room in the top photo is littered with wooden planks. The room in the middle photo is clear of wreckage. In the bottom photo, the cage lamp is nearly buried in silt.

Above: China ware lies among fallen panels.

Below: China bowl lid with the shipping line flag.

OLIVE BRANCH

1871 to 1880 September 30
92 feet in length
Wooden-hulled schooner
Maximum depth is 100 feet

This is another wreck that falls into the "cute" category. Below and bottom right: Fallen masts offer an opportunity to observe platform construction and step assembly.

Top right: A bilge pump with one of the wooden handles.
Above left: The wooden helm with a curious arrangement.
Above right: The planks have fallen off the bulwark. The railing is supported in part by the chainplates.

Books by the Author

Fiction

Vietnam
Lonely Conflict

Action/Adventure
Memory Lane
Mind Set

Supernatural
The Lurking

Science Fiction
Entropy
Return to Mars
Silent Autumn
The Time Dragons Trilogy
A Time for Dragons
Dragons Past
No Future for Dragons

Nonfiction

Advanced Wreck Diving Guide
Ultimate Wreck Diving Guide
Shipwrecks of Delaware and Maryland (1990)
Track of the Gray Wolf
Shipwrecks of New Jersey
Wilderness Canoeing

Order the titles listed below directly from:
GARY GENTILE PRODUCTIONS
P.O. Box 57137
Philadelphia, PA 19111
Shipping: $3 per order (not per book)

Deadeye jack-o'-lantern on the *City of Sheboygan*.

Nonfiction

$25 *Andrea Doria: Dive to an Era* (hard cover)
$20 *The Nautical Cyclopedia*
$20 *USS San Diego: the Last Armored Cruiser*
$20 *Wreck Diving Adventures*
$20 *Primary Wreck Diving Guide*
$30 *The Technical Diving Handbook*
$30 *Great Lakes Shipwrecks: a Photographic Odyssey*

Civil War ironclad ***Monitor***

$25 Book (hard cover) *Ironclad Legacy: Battles of the USS Monitorr*
$25 Videotape (NTSC/VHS): *The Battle for the USS Monitor*

The ***Lusitania*** Controversies (hard covers)
(These two volumes cover the evolution of wreck-diving from 1955 to 1995)

$25 Book One: *Atrocity of War and a Wreck-Diving History*
$25 Book Two: *Dangerous Descents into Shipwrecks and Law*

The Popular Dive Guide Series

$20 *Shipwrecks of New York*
$20 *Shipwrecks of New Jersey: North*
$20 *Shipwrecks of New Jersey: Central*
$20 *Shipwrecks of New Jersey: South*
$20 *Shipwrecks of Delaware and Maryland* (2002 Edition)
$20 *Shipwrecks of Virginia*
$20 *Shipwrecks of North Carolina: from the Diamond Shoals North*
$20 *Shipwrecks of North Carolina: from Hatteras Inlet South*
$20 *Shipwrecks of South Carolina and Georgia*

Wreck Diving Adventure Novel

$20 *The Peking Papers* (hard cover)

Order books and pay by credit card from the GGP website:

http://www.ggentile.com